THE ANXIETY DIARIES

Amy J Young

Copyright © 2024 by Amy J Young
All rights reserved.

No portion of this book may be reproduced in any form without written permission from the author.
It is sold with the understanding that neither the author nor the publisher is engaged in rendering legal, health, mental health or any other professional services in relation to any of the subject matter.
While the publisher and author have used their best efforts in preparing this book, they make no representations or warranties concerning the accuracy or completeness of the book's contents. The advice and strategies contained herein may not be suitable for your situation, and if you are experiencing severe anxiety, you should consult with a professional.
Neither the publisher nor the author shall be liable for any loss of profit or other commercial damages, including but not limited to special, incidental, consequential, personal, or other damages.

THE ANXIETY DIARIES

BOOK ONE

THE MIND

Contents

Disclaimer	1
Acknowledgement	3
Forward	5
1 A Letter to Anxiety	7
2 An Introduction To My Anxiety Journey	9
PART ONE	15
3 Recognising Anxiety	17
4 Triangle Trigger Theory	21
5 Dear Anxiety	27
PART TWO	33
6 Honesty	35
7 Open-Mindedness	39
8 Willingness	43
9 Forgiveness	47
10 Unity	51
11 Discipline	55
12 Faith	59

13 Responsibility	67
14 Love	73
15 Wholeness	79
16 Joy	83
17 Peace	87
18 Outwards	91
Resources	97

Disclaimer

I am NOT a trained professional doctor, counsellor or psychologist. This book is based on my own journey through anxiety and is completely based on my own opinions. I do not give medical advice, and anyone reading this should consider if any of its material is right for you. If you require help, please speak to a professional and reach out to someone.

You belong here.

Acknowledgement

I wish to thank all the people whom I have met along my journey, who have both consciously and unconsciously supported me through my anxiety journey, whether they realised it or not! You have helped me more than you will ever truly know.

To my amazingly supportive family, and extended family, for always being there for me. My mum, for your encouraging words and for cheering me on through every step of this book. My brother for your advice, that helped me to the finish line of writing this book.

My husband for your love through the good, rough and tough times. You always have my back.

My children, stepchildren, and little grandy, for being the reason I do anything and everything in life. You have all taught me more about life than I can even begin to express with words alone.

To my incredible friends, I see you all like family, and your love and support has always helped me through every situation!

I would also like to thank the Everyday Lightworker Practitioner Training family, for your valuable teachings and for opening my mind to an extraordinary new way of possibility.

And to YOU dear reader - if this book helps even one person in any way, then I will truly know that this labour of love has been worth it. Thank you, for choosing to spend your time reading this labour of love.

Forward

I am proud to say I am finally on the other side of my anxiety. I have completely turned my life around. I no longer experience panic attacks (it has been years since the last attack) and when anxiety does enter my world again, I can now deal with it very quickly.

For me, this was a long journey. I had so much to learn before I could get to this point.

Though everyone's journey is different, I hope this book helps you in some way. Even if you may only implement one example from this book, then my whole anxiety adventure will be well worth it for me. I remember how debilitating anxiety felt in my own experiences, and I want everyone to know that there can be a life without angst.

This book is the first of a three-part series. Each depicts what I believe, based on my own experiences, to be the three most important aspects to consider when working with anxiety. They are each as important as the other.

This book, Book One: The Mind, consists of two parts. Part One focuses on what I believe anxiety is and it's possible triggers. We delve into why I chose the 'Mind' first, and how I have come to understand that this is only one of three major aspects of anxiety. Part Two is a journey of exercises that, when implemented into your life, will help support your anxiety, in a unique way.

Before we start though, I feel it is important that you know this first:

We are ALWAYS a beautiful work in progress no matter what stage of our journey in life we are at!

As we progress in life, we uncover one layer only to reveal deeper ones. We continuously meet various obstacles in life that can be perceived as either good or bad. That is a part of life. With the exercises I share in this three-part series, having trialled them first-hand, I feel I am now much stronger on this anxiety journey to be able to move through the obstacles I meet along the way, so much quicker.

Am I perfect? Hell no!

Do situations still surprise me? Absolutely!

All I can do is continue to grow, to be myself, and to love myself even more. But the best part now? Anxiety no longer debilitates me, it liberates me!

And you can be liberated by anxiety too!

Let me show you how!

1

A Letter to Anxiety

Dear Anxiety,

I remember the days when you crept into my life ever so slowly and silently but then unleashed your wrath with such violent force that you turned my whole world upside down. Literally.

I remember the night I fainted on the living room floor and waking up having felt like it was all a dream, a hallucination, a life that was not my own.

I remember the day you sent me to hospital. The ride in the ambulance was such a blur that it had felt like an out-of-body experience. I felt like I was watching the whole situation outside of my own body, completely out of control but forced to watch the downward spiral of what I thought would be my demise.

Little did I know that these moments were turning points in my life. At the time it was frightening and I felt utterly alone but now I can look back and see it as a pivotal point in my journey thus far.

Anxiety, as much as I loathed you at the time, you have taught me to love myself and be the person I always wanted to be. Finally.

Thank you!

Yours sincerely,

Me, Amy - a recovering anxiety warrior

P.S. If I knew then what I know now, would I still have gone on this journey??

Absolutely!

***

Flash back to 2005 when I was first diagnosed with anxiety. My family doctor handed me a Doctor's Certificate to give to my family and workplace so I could take time off to get some much-needed rest.

His diagnosis; 'anxiety'.

I ignored it. I hid the certificate, amongst a pile of other papers, and then went on with my life.

***

2

An Introduction To My Anxiety Journey

It was a slow start to my anxiety. No one talked about it in 2005. I thought my doctor had used it as a simple diagnosis because he didn't know what was wrong with me. I shoved down the feelings and moved on. Back then my anxiety only popped up here and there so I would always just shrug it off. It didn't last too long, and I would either wait for it to pass or distract myself. What I didn't know then was that it was just biding its time. Year after year it started to creep in more and more. It wasn't until 2011 when it became more obvious, then in 2012 it hit me hard with my first real panic attack. I guess my anxiety had finally had enough of being ignored and was no longer making small requests. It had now started making big demands.

I woke up in the middle of the night with my heart racing, a tightening chest and shallow breathing. I got up out of bed slowly and walked to the bathroom. I remember seeing stars in my eyes, everything becoming quiet and then blacking out. I woke up on the lounge room floor to my husband standing over me. I told him I was fine and went back to bed.

I felt dizzy the next day and booked in to see my doctor after work. Maybe it was a concussion, I thought, not knowing anything about concussions, but blaming it on the head knock from the previous night. I made it to my lunch break at work and was standing in the staff kitchen when I started feeling dizzy again. My heart was pounding, my chest felt tight, and I was struggling to breathe. I started to panic and began hyperventilating. My work colleague walked in and could immediately see something was wrong. She lay me down, and all I remember is faint voices. It was like I wasn't even in my body anymore. They had called an ambulance, but even those details are still very blurry to me.

I finally came back to my body while in the hospital waiting bay. My blood sugar levels had been very low. My blood pressure was low too. That was the cause of the symptoms they had said, it was the panic that had sent me over the top.

Thinking back about the months that led to these two events above, I remember I had started to become restless at night and struggled to sleep often. I would hyper-fixate on something someone had said or done and I would replay it in my mind over and over again. I would scare myself over every worst-case scenario I could think of and would dread the thought of upsetting someone, or even worse, letting someone down. I would say yes to everyone and every job at work. I would bend over backwards to help any family or friends, even if I was too exhausted already. I struggled to say no. I was often tense, worried, stuck in my mind and struggled to feel at ease. I was burnt out, overworked and completely overstimulated. My mind, body, and soul were depleted.

What happened after these two events was worse. I would experience periods where the anxiety became so severe that I would be too nervous to travel, even by car to somewhere close, or to leave the house for fear of blacking out. I struggled with heights and would feel shaky in any building or structure above two floors or more. I would become dizzy in either a confined space, or what felt like its polar opposite, a massive open space. I felt tense with sudden changes in lights and any sudden loud sounds. I avoided elevators, main roads, tunnels, highways, planes, cinemas and anything that felt like I could potentially be stuck with no easy way out. Sometimes I would be pushed into unavoidable situations, and when I had to face these fears I would feel those similar symptoms starting to peak. Some days I would be ok and could work up the courage to face them, others I was a nervous wreck. It would take all my energy to keep myself from panicking in front of people, or I would find myself trying to distract myself so I could get through my day. Often I would excuse myself as quickly as possible, to get to a safe spot to breathe it out until I could function again.

I cried often. I couldn't understand how these simple things I used to do all the time, had somehow now become increasingly hard! How could some days be ok facing these normal day-to-day events, and then others I would see myself falling apart? I would try to hide it as much as possible from my work colleagues, family, and friends. I was embarrassed, ashamed, and felt completely alone. I constantly felt exhausted, but had to force myself to put on a happy face each day.

My weight dropped noticeably. Over the years I was diagnosed with other conditions, such as Chronic Fatigue Syndrome, Hypoglycemia, and of course, anxiety. I tried medical test after test, as I did NOT want to have anxiety. I wanted it to be something else, something I could get rid of quickly!

On the outside, I tried to remain positive and in control. On the inside, I was falling apart.

My doctor was amazing. He went along with every idea I had about my health, but he gently kept bringing me back to the diagnosis of anxiety and exhaustion. I was way too busy to rest, and I was working so hard that I certainly didn't feel as though I could take a break! I tried many different diets to get the exhaustion under control. This worked for a little while, but, anxiety would always creep back in again.

In 2014, I met Michelle Lightworker and the incredible people at Lightworker Reflections, who introduced me to the 12 Everyday Lightworker Principles. This opened my world to meditation, and seeing myself, and my life, from a new perspective. From the inside out. From this experience, I started to pursue my love of writing. I was encouraged to write about what I was going through and had the opportunity to share them through the Lightworker Advocate Magazine. A dear friend who I met through my Everyday Lightworker Practitioner studies, also had anxiety, and together we both wrote about our anxious moments in a way that would speak directly to our anxiety, and 'The Anxiety Diaries', were born.

My confidence grew by sharing my experiences in written form. The more I wrote, the more I started to understand my anxiety. I would ask myself questions, and what would flow out onto the pages, would not only help me, but other people would respond in thanks for my words. Writing was therapeutic and healing. I would find my answers in my writing. Often it was as if my anxiety spoke for itself while I was in writing mode.

As I look back over the years, from then to now, the last few years my anxiety was up and down. I would come so far and feel great, then something unexpected would happen then down I would go again. The more I wrote to my anxiety, the more layers I would peel back. The more I researched and worked on myself, the more answers I would reveal.

Today I am predominantly free of anxiety. I no longer have panic attacks, and whenever I do feel anxiety beginning to creep in, I know how to deal with it quickly. Anxiety no longer stops me for more than a few minutes. I am incredibly proud of myself, and of the journey I have taken alongside my anxiety. It may have taken much longer than I had ever hoped, but it has helped shape the person I am today and I AM proud of the person I am.

So my intention here is to share with others a different way of looking at anxiety. I am not a trained professional. I am not a doctor, I am not a psychologist, nor am I a counsellor. I am a regular person who has had anxiety. I have tried the services of many different professionals over the years and each has been helpful in one way or another. If you do need help, I always recommend seeing a trained professional. Your life here is needed. You have your journey in front of you and are meant to be here. Please see someone if you have suicidal or harmful thoughts. Please!

In the beginning, I never would have thought that I could look back one day and see my anxiety in a different light. But now, I am thankful for my anxiety. Having anxiety was the best thing to happen to me! It was not a burden, it was my wake-up call.

Anxiety has changed my life, for the better.

PART ONE

3

Recognising Anxiety

Not everyone has the same anxiety symptoms, not everyone has the same experience with anxiety, and there is no one, single, simple solution that works for everyone.

However, I do believe in a life with less anxiety, and yes, even a life with hardly any anxiety at all! This was my driving force. As much as I hated life at the time, through every anxious experience, I remember a time when I had predominantly lived without it. I knew in my heart that I could either get to the end of my anxiety or if not, live with it in a way that would no longer hold me back from living life the way I wanted. I would not, and will never, accept that that was the way it would be forever.

After years of trialling everything I had researched, and years of closely observing my anxiety, I learned that I could measure my anxiety in two stages.

Stage one: a slow build-up of angst, filled with many types of symptoms that would cause quite an agonising experience that would last for minutes or sometimes even days!

Stage two: an insane rush that happened extremely quickly, and for me would last usually only a few minutes. Although rushed, at the time it felt like the end of the world.

Both stages are serious, and I have witnessed other people experience these two stages as well. The second stage can be very frightening for not only the person with the anxiety but also anyone watching and not knowing what is happening or what to do.

I have explained these two stages in more detail below, however, please remember that not all people experience anxiety the same way. Some may experience a handful of these symptoms, others may experience a range of a few below along with others I have not covered at all. I am merely documenting my own experiences and those I have witnessed of others.

Stage 1. The Anxiety Experience

I call it an experience as that is what it is to me, moments in my life where I was feeling very anxious. Feeling tight chested, a lump in the throat, nausea, feeling confined, the mind going in spirals thinking of every possible who, what, where, and when scenario.

From the outside it may look like the person is stuck in daydream mode, often stiffened or pacing and/or fidgeting, not engaging fully in the present moment. Often moving from room to room or many trips outside for fresh air, followed by sleepless nights with the mind constantly racing.

Note: - *Some people are amazing at masking this stage. My clinical psychologist once told me that I could win an Academy Award for my ability to show the world I was ok on the surface!*

For myself, I would often sit quite rigidly still, clenching my teeth and lost deep in thought of every outrageous scenario. I would try to slowly breathe through my tight chest, the lump in my throat, or the sickly butterflies. This could last hours or even days, depending on what the situation was. Sometimes it would build slowly, and just remain there, agonisingly plaguing me until the situation changed.

Stage 2. The Panic Attack
This is exactly how it sounds. An attack of sheer panic. Feeling like I could no longer breathe, hyperventilating, a sudden change in body temperature, feeling as though I was about to vomit, then, as if I was about to faint, or if I didn't faint, it was extreme dizziness and/or an emotional breakdown at the moment. It was hard to speak, communicate or even think rationally. Complete overwhelm. Wanting to run or crawl into a hiding place, but feeling frozen and heavy.

It takes a lot of energy to pull yourself out of this point. The timeline could be different for each person, but for me, it was usually a matter of minutes - that felt like forever… I would be extremely exhausted after each panic attack.

If you have experienced these stages quite differently, I would be very interested in hearing how these two stages affect you, so that I can be more helpful and understanding when relating to others. Please feel free to share your experience with me. As I mentioned previously, anxiety is not the same for everyone. I completely respect that.

If you are reading this and have never experienced anxiety, I hope this gives you a deeper understanding of how someone you may know may be experiencing anxiety. To watch someone you love go through this, particularly full-on panic attacks, as they can be quite scary.

To every person who has pulled themselves out of an anxiety experience or panic attack, whether assisted or not, you are incredible! The amount of courage and energy it can take to do so is nothing short of a warrior. Be proud of yourself!

Thank you for choosing to still be here.

4

Triangle Trigger Theory

I journal a lot. Not like in a set routine type of way. Mainly just notes, comments, long meaningful phrases, or doodles when I have a lot on my mind. Writing has always helped soothe me and that is most likely the reason I had always wanted to be an author.

I remember back to a time when I was journalling about a recent anxiety experience and the very real, physical symptoms that I had felt. What had triggered my anxiety in those moments? How did I feel in those moments? What symptoms did I experience?

As I was listing all the recent situations, I realised that I didn't have one specific reason for my anxiety triggering, I had many! They started pouring out of me as I went through all the experiences I could remember. Some of them followed similar themes, so I started grouping my experiences, and I found that my triggers came down to three main recurring headings.

Mind

- When my mind could not turn off to all the what ifs
- The thought of being trapped in a certain situation
- Continuous thought spirals playing over and over of what could happen in the future
- Replaying a past situation like a movie on loop
- Thoughts of what could happen during the suspense before an event was about to unfold

Body

- Physical body symptoms like dizziness, exhaustion, tight chested
- Feelings of overwhelm, overstimulated, too exerted or even too excited!
- Hunger, hormonal, feeling faint or sick to the stomach, butterflies, etc
- Emotional dysregulation
- Physically reacting the same way in certain situations out of habit either knowingly or unknowingly

Soul

- Anxiety brought on by compromised personal boundaries and morals
- The feeling of not belonging
- Lost in my life purpose

- Feeling caged in life
- Past hurt or traumas resurfacing
- Unconscious programs and patterns when constantly triggered by the same situations and can't seem to shift it.

The Mind/Body/Soul concept is used in many teachings worldwide for various reasons and is not a new idea, however, I had never seen it applied to anxiety. I was surprised that I could look at each experience on my list, and how I felt at those times and was able to put them into one of those three themes. I drew a triangle and labelled it with these three concepts for anxiety, and kept it where I could see it.

I realised that if either one of these Mind / Body / Soul concepts were out of balance then anxiety would start to build. Sometimes it could be a combination of the three, however, I slowly learned to identify which one it was more clearly over time. In each anxiety experience, I would ask myself *"Which trigger am I working with here? Mind, Body or Soul?"* As I practised this question, I became faster and faster at identifying which part was out of balance as anxiety began, and how to react before it became a panic attack.

The other silver lining with this question is that I quickly learned what my pre-symptoms for anxiety were for each trigger (yes they are each slightly different), how to recognise the main trigger quickly, and how to apply the right support to bring myself back into balance.

Everything started to make sense when I figured out how this Triangle Trigger Theory applied to my anxiety. I realised that I required different types of support for each area. I needed to retrain my MIND to be more open to new solutions, I needed to work with my BODY so it received the care it requires to run optimally, and I needed to understand myself at a holistic SOUL level to truly know myself and to regain trust in myself.

I am going to share with you the exercises I used to strengthen each area in the hope that it may just help someone else. This book, the first of a three-part series, is all about the MIND. I will delve into The Body and The Soul in the following two books.

This series starts with the mind as we need our mind on board with us on this journey, and it helps to have its complete support before we start heading deeper into the body and soul work. If the mind is still dragging you down thought spirals and leading you back to fear, then it can make working with the other aspects a little more challenging. There is no wrong or right way to do this but after going back and forth through all the triggers I found starting with the mind has helped me the most.

The mind for me was one of my most noticeable triggers at first. After observing my behaviours through my writing and meditations, I could see how I was stuck in these thought spirals often. But I didn't know how to stop them or how to move through them. Once I started working with the mind, I then learned that under these mind triggers, there was at times a body or soul trigger hiding under them too. Sometimes even both! So, starting with the mind is the best place to begin so that it can be ready to support us as we dive deeper.

In the next part of this book, Part Two, I have shared several exercises with you as each works in its own very special way. There are 12 chapters total within Part Two, and each chapter is a step away from having severe anxiety and a step towards finding peace with yours! Yes, peace with anxiety! Stay with me through these chapters because not only might you find peace, but you will also understand why I believe that anxiety is a superpower!

Yes, you read that right.

Anxiety is a superpower!

Take a breath, buckle up, and let's start the MIND journey together!

*The 12 chapters that begin Part 2 of this book, Honesty to Peace, are based on my experiences during my training on the 12 Everyday Lightworker Principles through the Everyday Lightworker Practitioner Training. What I learned from these principles, prompted me to write many journal entries. The following chapters are based on these entries and how I felt they related to my anxiety. I have only merely touched the surface of how healing these principles can be within this book, but they are so much more than this. I have added some resources at the end of this book, for those who wish to source more information about these amazing Principles.

5

Dear Anxiety

I have a friend named anxiety
She often likes to sit with me
Her body is hunched
Worry written on her face
She sways ever so slowly
Gazing out into space

I ask her to tell me all the things on her mind
She looks at me fearfully with pain-filled eyes
I open my arms and I hold her there
She slides into panic and utters words of despair

She worries about the past with so much sorrow
She worries about the impact it will have on tomorrow
She tries to think rationally and be one step ahead
In preparation for all the outcomes held in her head

It's all become too much

She is drowning in stress
She wants to run and hide
And be free of this mess

As her breath becomes rapid
I ask her to slow
She shakes her head angrily
And explains how it goes

Her heart beats too fast
Her throat is so dry
Her body feels heavy
Her eyes try to cry
But she cannot move
Her feet chained to the ground
She can no longer hear
She can't make a sound

I see her mind thinking
Spiraling fast
She is deciding her next move
Fight or flight is her path
I hold her hand tight
And pull her hand to my heart
I tell her that here is the best place to start
I hold her gaze strong
And invite her to breathe
Her hand on my heart
Feels the rhythm she needs
I show her this moment

The presence of now
She settles into her body
As it breathes in and out

We find where anxiety
In her body is stored
We breathe fresh air
Into it's energetic core

We acknowledge that anxiety
Is an emotion so real
But all it wants is for the body
To be still and to feel

As we feel it together
And ask it why
It starts to respond
It lets out a cry
Confronting the pain
That was hiding so deep
And finally acknowledged
It could now be released
The mind is so strong
But needed a rest
The heart tried to tell it
But the head thought it knew best

Anxiety had wanted to help everyone
By holding their worries so they could have fun
She sheltered those around her from pain and from fear

And held it to her close
So she could save all their tears

But as she held them one by one
Her body would become more overrun
Until one day her body had just had enough
She could no longer feel joy
Had no room to feel love

Anxiety screamed and finally released
All the pain she had held
With every heartbeat

It is ok to offer
others her help
but only after she had taken care of herself

If she filled her own cup
She would have plenty to share
As long as she replenished it
With self-love and self-care

I hugged my friend anxiety
And told her I was proud
For this loving new knowledge
that she had courageously found
I whispered
Remember
If you ever feel down
All you need is to breathe in this moment

Right here
Right now

- **Amy J Young**

PART TWO

6

Honesty

HONESTLY, HONESTY IS THE BEST PLACE TO START

Sometimes the hardest step in doing anything is to start somewhere. Just thinking about working through anxiety can be overwhelming so I am going to make this first exercise as straightforward as possible.

BE... COMPLETELY... HONEST ... WITH...YOURSELF!

"I experience anxiety....and that's ok!" Say it out loud. Feels a little lighter right?

For years I chased medical test after medical test for my diagnosis to be something different and it wasn't until one doctor, of the many I had spoken to, sat me down and thoroughly explained anxiety to me – "Amy, you have severe anxiety!". Hearing these words, I felt shocked, embarrassed, and even ashamed! I had so many physical and very real symptoms. How could anxiety be the answer? It was a hard and uncomfortable truth to swallow for me but as I processed the information over and over, I finally accepted that he was right.

I was finally honest with the most important person in my life, ME.

Being honest with yourself about your feelings, your current situation, and how you have arrived at this exact moment in time, can be very confronting. To be present with all of you, right here and right now in all your feelings takes courage and commitment to truly look. It can be very uncomfortable to see the REAL you and even more uncomfortable to feel your TRUE feelings. However, I knew that I could not go on trying to be different or even trust myself fully again if I wasn't completely honest with myself right now.

This is WHO I am right now, this is HOW I am right now and this is MY journey to this moment right now.

Own it. The good, the bad, and yes the very ugly. I wanted the panic attacks to end and this was the first step. Being one hundred percent completely honest with myself!

TRY THIS:

Either write/video/talk to yourself in the mirror or record your voice and be completely honest with yourself about you and only YOU! All of it. The anger, the frustration, the sadness, absolutely anything about your anxiety. Put it all on the table. No one else needs to read, hear, or see this. You do not have to share or edit it, or even ever review it again after this moment. Whatever comes out does not even have to make sense. Just be yourself, taking time out to be truly honest with yourself.

NOTE: You can return to this exercise whenever you need to. You can make new entries anytime you feel it might help. It takes practice to start being honest with ourselves. If you are someone like me who has hidden from your feelings, tried to be someone else, and worn different masks to please people, then do not feel bad if you have to do this exercise a few times until it becomes brutally natural. I still use it in many situations today when I feel overwhelmed, frustrated or angry as it helps me to understand where I haven't been truthful to myself or my boundaries. Getting it out of my head, off my chest and onto some paper, or any other way outside of my mind, means that I am lightening some of the mental load by breaking my spiralling thought cycle.

Please don't read on yet. Please do this exercise. Make some time to do it however you can. I would write in the car whilst waiting to pick up kids from school or wake up in the middle of the night when I couldn't sleep (from my anxiety) and write it all down in point form. Whatever works best for you. You don't always need a lot of time, but I would recommend doing this exercise within a dedicated timeslot for yourself, you could even do this with someone who you trust, who can just be there with you and who won't intervene or interrupt you.

This may be the first step, but for me, it is often the hardest!

Afterwards please take some time to just breathe, go for a walk, drink lots of water or eat something that will bring you back. Shedding a lot of truth is big energetic work. Take it easy on yourself after this.

7

Open-Mindedness

BEING OPEN TO SOMETHING NEW

The thing I have learned about anxiety is that we tend to look to the past or the future. We are so good at looking at an issue from every negative angle, and working out every worst-case scenario that could possibly go wrong. It's a bit of a talent, really. This can help in some situations but it can also become a form of self-sabotage and keep you from creating positive change and moving forward.

One of the most important quotes I have learned on this journey -

"You cannot solve a problem with the same mind that created it." - Albert Einstein.

Boom! That one always hits home for me.

After being honest with myself, I learned how easily I could get stuck in the mind spiral of trying to deal with all the scenarios that could go wrong. It would start with one thought, then off I would go into a long spate of "what ifs" until I was unable to move or breathe under the weight of it. This is where teaching myself to be open-minded helped me beyond ways I could not understand at the time. I knew that to be able to overcome some of my anxiety challenges, I had to learn that change was ok, and that it was only going to happen if I was open to changing the way I previously thought and acted. I wanted to completely flip my world around. So, that is what I did! When I started to feel anxious in certain situations, I learned to be more open-minded by flipping it around.

I created what I like to call, the **'What Could Go Right?'** game.

Turning away from what could go wrong and being both curious and courageous to explore what could go right! It has taken much practice, and sometimes I still catch myself in the worst-case scenario spiral! *(Hey we are always a beautiful work in progress right?)* Learning to spend more time exploring best-case scenarios, can get as wild and crazy as the worst-case ones! The difference is, I feel much clearer, confident and supported. It shifts that heaviness feeling much quicker!

Note: I don't dismiss that there could be uncomfortable moments, feelings of fear, or the arrival of information I am not aware of yet, BUT choosing to spend more energy on exploring more positive solutions means I am more open-minded to the many, many, more new options available.

It also blows my mind when a solution drops in that I never would have even dreamed was possible, and yet, it is more perfect than I could have realised! I only needed to be more open-minded to receive it.

TRY THIS:

I have been training myself for a while now to flip my mind into what could be the best-case scenarios when I am worried, stressed, or anxious. It does take practice but you can do this! Worrying about something before it has happened, if it even happens at all, means using up more energy and being more exhausted. When you catch yourself feeling anxious about a situation say out loud all the things that can go right. It can be big things or small things. Even if they feel not so right at the time, still keep going and create a positive thought spiral which helps to replace the negative one. I try to get at least 10 or more "go rights", no matter what they are! It's the momentum that begins to break the cycle, so the more, the better! This may feel strange or awkward at first as it is a big change in the way you have done this before. However, it has helped me through so many situations and I did not use up as much energy and time worrying, and instead I can only be thankful for having used it and becoming more present in my life.

This game is a game-changer. It is not only working with anxiety, it is training you to be more optimistic and to positively seek out new solutions in all areas of life. We often keep trying to meet our challenges with our old ways of doing them. This game helps you to explore new ways and to make that a new habit. As Einstein said, you cannot change problems with the same mind that created them. Dare to be more open-minded!

8

Willingness

WHEN WE WANT TO CHANGE BUT DO NOT KNOW HOW

WILLINGNESS *(noun) - the quality or state of being prepared to do something - Dictionary.com*

It's one thing to WANT to change your world but it's another thing to be WILLING to do it.

Whilst in my head I can dream up all the amazing desires and experiences I want to have in my world but to then make those changes in real life felt challenging, difficult, and even scary! I wanted to no longer feel caged in my anxious world but the thought of making any changes would have me feeling anxiety. Stepping out of any of my comfort zones meant I was met with panic attacks, dizziness and a feeling of shortness of breath.

I would get so frustrated at myself for being this way, even over simple little things like avoiding fun plans, just so I didn't have to feel anxious. I would go back to the self-loathing of being stuck. It felt like my thoughts and my body would turn against me. Why was this happening to me?!

A friend asked me one day if I was willing to change. "OF COURSE I AM" I replied but she explained, "Not just WANTING to change, are you WILLING to change?"

I thought about this a lot and pulled it apart in every way I could to fully understand what she meant. I realised for me it meant this: willing to change means that I am willing to do the work within myself to change. It meant that I didn't just want to change and leave it at that, I was willing to do whatever I needed to, to change. I would have to be honest with myself not just be open-minded to change, but actually be willing to DO the change. Well honestly, at first I was triggered by this big time! I was not in a position to just jump out of my safety zone and be ok with it. No way could I just change from having anxiety to not having anxiety! What if I panicked? What if I fainted?

So to help myself be ok with doing the work I needed to do to make the change, I settled for the following:
"I am willing, to be willing, to change my life". Yes, that felt a little lighter and much less overwhelming.

When we accept and choose to try to change we take the pressure off ourselves from the overwhelming thoughts of having to make a huge change all at once. Those thoughts stop us in the first place, because it feels too hard, too risky or too big. It's one little step first, followed by a succession of little steps that make the outcome appear. If I continue to stay committed to my willingness to change I know that every little step is at least one more little step towards a bigger and better picture. One little step closer than I was before.

TRY THIS:
Write down the things that you WANT to change. After this line write, I AM WILLING to be WILLING TO CHANGE THIS. Then put this in a place where you can refer back to it often.

When I am going through a tough situation, or being annoyed at myself that something hasn't changed yet, I tell myself "I am willing to be willing to change this" It's like a little pep talk to keep me going no matter where I am at. It also breaks the negative thought cycle of 'this is too hard, or too big" to putting it into, "it's ok to take baby steps" mode.

Little steps are a part of every process in almost anything in life! Once those little steps become habit they turn into easier steps over time. Like a rolling snowball in those old cartoons. It starts as a teeny tiny snowball, then builds momentum, adding more snow on every rotation, and finally, it has grown so huge and so powerful that it can destroy anything in its path! Never underestimate little steps!

9

Forgiveness

FORGIVING THE MOST IMPORTANT PERSON IN MY LIFE

This is one big topic and so important in this part of the journey. I won't go into the full ins and out of forgiveness because seriously, I would need a whole book on this one topic. I will touch on this in the later stages of writing these books but for the MIND book we start with, what I feel, is the first layer of forgiveness in relation to anxiety.

Forgiveness of Self.

When I learned about forgiveness I always thought it was about forgiving others or seeking others to forgive me. I never really thought too much about forgiving myself. I could recall many moments where I felt I had done wrong to others who I hoped had forgiven me, and many moments I hoped others would apologise to me, however, I did not know how to forgive myself. Whilst all of these types of forgiveness are important in their own right, this chapter works with self-forgiveness, and in particular, our anxiety.

I wrote the word layers above, as yes, there are many layers to all stages of healing. The first three chapters are focused on preparing yourself to get into some of the deeper work. Taking these steps one at a time helps to do so in a non-rushed and gentle way. Layer by layer. It's like anything you take on, there is always a start and always a process with seeing results, as long as you are willing to commit to each step! If there is one step you actually do take from this book, I hope it is this one! This is the one that helped me going forward. This chapter takes a little imagination on your part, but it has helped me more than I can ever explain.

The Anxiety Diaries for me was born from many journal entries, meditations, and speaking with my anxiety. I would separate myself from my anxiety and visualise this part of myself as its own being.

For me, she would be floating slowly, a very quiet, withdrawn version of myself with large eyes, hunched over. I would ask her why she was so anxious, why she made me feel this way or why she was ruining my life! Sometimes I received answers, often I did not. Sometimes I was so angry and would yell and scream at her, other times I would just cry or simply ignore her. Sometimes the visualisations would change, reshape or change colours. There were times when she appeared as a child version of myself and I would simply just hold her.

One meditation, I was asked if I could forgive her. Could I forgive all the anxious moments in my life? Could I forgive myself for being anxious, could I forgive myself for having anxiety and could I forgive all the situations where I experienced anxiety? It came as a huge feeling in my chest, it was like this heavy weight that for me was a huge black box. Each time I said the words "I forgive you", I saw the block slowly chipping away, crumbling. I forgave myself for the ways I acted when anxious, I forgave myself for just trying to survive through my anxiety,

I forgave myself for the things I said when anxious and I forgave my anxiety for feeling the way it did. I FORGAVE MYSELF.

After each visualisation and journal entry, I began to feel so much lighter. As moments of anxiety would creep back in over the days, I would whisper to myself, "I forgive you, anxiety"

By learning to see my anxiety as a person that needed love and attention I began to treat it the way I would if this was someone I loved e.g. a child, a best friend, a family member or even a pet. The power of this visualisation is indescribable and changed everything for me and my anxiety. I started to acknowledge myself and see myself as worthy of my attention. I had never really done this before. It was like a veil had been lifted and there was this person inside who was real and this person needed attention from the most important person in their life! Me! I finally stopped hating her and realised she needed me. She needed me more than anyone else did. I finally met the person I had been ignoring for years and anxiety was how she got my attention. Forgiving myself was truly a gift.

TRY THIS:
Visualise your anxiety as a unique part of you. Describe how it looks, acts, and feels. It's ok if it changes, or does not look like you, or even human! Maybe it's a shape or a colour. There is no wrong way to do this. Then either write to it, talk to it or sit in stillness with this part of you. It's important to recognise it and acknowledge it. Take some time on this process and let it unfold in a timely way for you. When you are ready, and only when you are ready, start to forgive your anxiety. It may not happen the first time and may even take a few tries to

do this. "I forgive you", are powerful words. Write it, say it, feel it. "I forgive you", "I forgive myself", or "I forgive you, anxiety". Then each time anxiety comes up for you after this exercise, can you whisper to yourself, I forgive you.

10

Unity

I AM NOT ALONE

Loneliness is the feeling I often feel when experiencing anxiety. People who cared about me would try to be supportive but I knew they didn't really understand what I was feeling. Looking back now I feel like the loneliness was some of the toughest moments in my journey. It was hard to explain the real feelings to someone who didn't understand, so often I didn't say much at all.

This began to change when I started being honest with myself and started talking to different people about anxiety. I would hear someone say, "Oh my sister has that", or "My daughter has feelings like those", and then some people would turn up in different situations of my life and tell me that they have anxiety too! Books, magazines and social media posts opened my mind even further that there were people all over the world from different countries, backgrounds and all ages who also have anxiety. Wow! Even today as I sit here and write this page I am still reminded often of the magnitude of people who experience anxiety. Chances are, you dear reader, either experience anxiety yourself or you know someone who does! Yes, there are many of us!

Although I felt alone in the moments of my anxiety, I know now that I am not completely alone.

I started to imagine them all around the world. Different people, going about their lives with anxiety just like mine. I wanted to hold them all and tell them they were not alone. Tell them that I too had anxiety and know how it feels. I would tell them in my mind that they will get through this just like I am!

You are not alone in anxiety. There are many of us! Millions of us! All feeling alone in this together. If we could just reach out and find one another. We are all here. We all have a unique story to tell and we all have something to share in this world, even if we only get through to just one person, then to me, it is completely worth it. Let's not let others feel that they are alone with this!

This part of the journey is all about Unity! We are all one. We are connected. The power of unity is incredible. It gives us the strength to keep going. Strength to believe in ourselves and strength to get through this, for not only you, but others too. Even if we do not know them.

I will try to do this for those BEFORE me, those WITH me and those AFTER me.

TOGETHER WE GOT THIS.

TRY THIS:

I don't need to explain too much here because if you have read the page above then you may have guessed what to do. If you are feeling alone, know that you are not the only person with anxiety. You are not the first and you are not the last. You have a huge amount of people who, just like you, are trying to get through this. Find some time to tune in within and remind yourself you are not alone or you can simply look up many of the internet or social media groups with people who have experienced anxiety. They are out there. You are not completely alone in anxiety.

11

Discipline

WHEN DISCIPLINE FINALLY BECOMES A WORD I LOVE

Let's recap a little – we have been honest with ourselves about our anxiety, we have been open-minded to adapting to change, become willing to try to do the work to create the positive changes in our life, we have forgiven the most important person right now and we know we are not on this journey alone. Phew! That's a lot to take in! Well done if you are still with me here!

So, how do we physically make the changes, well, change more? I felt like I had tried for years to have that positive life without anxiety yet I was still there! I had tried countless exercises, diets, how-to books, seminars, doctors, and therapies and I was still having anxiety.

Enter the next phase – discipline! Now if your stomach just turned at this word then I don't blame you. When I first learned about the discipline concept I loathed this word. It reminded me of being a child and being scolded or having to stick to boring routines like budgets or diets that I didn't enjoy and never actually worked for me. Until I understood discipline in a new light. Discipline guides me to stay on track with my willingness to change. It does not force me to do anything I don't want to it reminds me to commit to what I do want in life.

Remember how we worked on being open-minded for new solutions to drop in and we wrote down all those changes we wanted in life that we were willing to be willing to change? Well, I believe that change happens from within first and then shows up in our outside world. If we are still in the same mindset we were before the change, then we are going to keep going the same way until we make some new serious mind habits.

So instead of writing routines and steps that I was to follow each day (*honestly I seriously struggle with routines and sameness day in and day out, hence the different exercises in this book*), I wanted my discipline to be something that would help me commit to creating positive anxiety changes in very small steps. Never anything overwhelming of course because that would become way too hard to keep on top of too. My usual actions each day were of fear, anxiety and trying so hard to please others. If I wanted positive change then I knew that I would have to flip this over in a way that did not feel like a chore but created longer positive mind habits so that I could recognise the new solutions when they revealed themselves. So I chose something I could commit to doing easily each day or as I remembered it so that it would quickly build to something that felt natural.

Introducing the What CAN Go Right game's next level - the What DID Go Right game! - Anxiety never saw this one coming!

Remember back in the open-minded challenge of pointing out all the things that COULD go right? Well, this time we are picking out what DID go right! During my anxiety it was really easy to dwell on all the things that seemed to be going wrong during the day – everything felt so hard, I always get the red lights, I hate this traffic, I drop everything, I am always last, I always miss out, nothing is going my way today, why am I so clumsy, I am so terrible at this, I feel trapped etc etc. So in true flip-the-mind fashion, every day I would quickly ramble off the things that DID go right. Usually just before I went to bed, that way I was setting myself up for a more positive sleep send-off rather than an anxious one worrying about all the stuff I didn't get to! Or I would set random reminders on my phone, and play it with my kids while standing in a queue, brushing my teeth or washing the dishes. In those moments that my mind needed some stimulation, I would be saying out loud all the things that DID go right.

TRY THIS:

Before you go to sleep tonight or during any of your mundane (or not mundane) chores, think of at least ten things that DID go right in the day. It can be anything big or small! Example: "I aced that angle park today" or "I got through a day not spilling anything on my clothes!" That was a great one for me! Do you get my point though? Pick out all the best moments no matter how silly they may seem. It can feel strange at first but it gets better over time!

Ready for Level 3? Once you get into a habit of doing this at random times, start to train yourself to do it straight after something does go right. Acknowledge it at the point it happens. This slowly becomes the normal thought pattern and gets our mind looking for all the good things in the day and not dwelling on the things that went wrong or could have gone wrong.

Sure, things still may seem like they go wrong, but the difference is we now don't spend too much time or energy on them anymore. You will be surprised how many things feel like they do go right when you actively start looking for them!

Now, if you are a real game player like me, level 4 of this game is flipping those wrong things into something good! Like me every time I slip over "Wow that was a fun ride!", or being stuck in traffic "I can use this time to chat to my friend or pretend I can sing", or spilling coffee on myself, "I am thankful I have a washing machine for these moments!" That reminds me of one of my favourite questions. When someone asks me if my cup is half full or half empty, I'm just glad to have a cup!

Discipline keeps me on track to committing to flipping my mind away from my usual old ways of thinking so that I am ready to take on new opportunities as they arise. I am willing to change and this is one small thing I can do often to bring more positive change into my life. The more I do this, the more confident I feel in life to make new decisions as I am looking for reasons for it to go right, and how it did go right! And now I have lots of examples, both big and small, to prove to myself that things do in fact, go right!

12

Faith

HAVE A LITTLE FAITH THIS MIGHT JUST WORK

Once we start the healing journey and the act of change in any situation, you may have likely in the past come up against a wall, an obstacle or what feels like a hard point. Maybe you are up against one right now? It's like you are zooming along doing so well and then all of a sudden it's a grinding halt at a huge STOP sign. An unexpected situation rears its head.

It feels like one step forward two steps back, right? Like you are saving money so well and have extra money coming in and then all of a sudden, bang, a big unexpected expense appears that puts you back to square one.

These moments can happen when you start to change. It helps me in these moments, to refer to this as 'taking out the dirty laundry'. I even call it this when it's happening. "Oh here's the last of my dirty laundry", time to throw out the last load of the old ways of doing things, and make space for the new!

Sometimes it's about clearing out the old 'stuff' from our old way of dealing with anxiety before a new open-minded perception can become permanent. Life presents you with an opportunity to show that you are ready to change and you can break this cycle by choosing how you deal with this situation differently from the way you have before.

Enter stage right - Faith.

Time to develop faith that it's OK to try something new. Faith that you can change, and are changing. Faith that you are on the right track and these moments are old patterns ready for new solutions much different to the past.

I know this is easier said than done, but when I started to have faith that no matter what this part of the journey looked like, I knew that I would get through this. I am here in this very moment right now after every challenge I have ever faced in the past. It may not be perfect right now but I have made it to this point. I knew that I had committed to change and I was willing to try to change and every moment is my opportunity!

As a person who had high anxiety, I used to feel like I needed to be in complete control of all situations. I didn't want to let anyone down or have any nasty surprises so I would try to control what was happening as much as I could. But I will let you in on something, I had to learn the long way round - *"I simply can't control every situation, I can't control others and I definitely cannot control their reactions. I can only choose MY reaction."* Once I accepted this it took a lot of pressure off myself to have to be perfect, in control or the need to please others so much.

Try this for a mind flip - if I am in complete control of everything that is unfolding, then chances are I am not being open-minded enough for a new solution to drop in to create those life changes that I want! Read that one again slowly! I need to have faith that situations will unfold whether I try to control them or not.

Whilst I don't need to have complete control, I do, however, have my choices. You have a choice here. It may not feel like you do but you have the choice to decide how you react to a situation. Will it be the way you have always reacted in the past or will it be a chance to choose a different reaction? Choosing the way you always have in the past means most likely similar results. Choosing to react differently means new opportunities for new solutions.

So what do I do right now, as I am faced with this big STOP sign?

I lean into faith that an answer will come to me in one way or another and I affirm that I am willing to be open-minded to a different solution to one I have used before. I am no longer letting my anxiety run the show, I am having faith that it will work out without my anxiety.

Faith helps me to move through these challenges knowing that they are just that, challenges, and they too will one day pass.

As I write this chapter I am sitting inside a country regional servo (gas/fuel service station) on a busy highway in Australia. It's raining so hard outside that I can no longer see the road in front of me. I knew that I really should stay off the road as it's not safe right now. I was on my way home to write this book, this very chapter, and I was at first, annoyed at the rain for getting in my way.

It's nice in here. It's quiet and I have a comfy place to sit. I have good coffee and food. It's dry. I pull out my phone and open my notes and here I am writing about faith! Had I driven home in this rain I would have been driving very slow and cautiously, or pulled over on the side of the highway to wait for it to stop. I would have been busy at home trying to bunker everything down in the rain and certainly not be writing this chapter! Here, in this comfy service station, I have the perfect safe surroundings, and even though I don't have my laptop I have another way to continue writing about the need to have faith and to let go of complete control of an outcome.

Even yesterday, being Valentine's Day I had organised a date for my husband and I (it was my turn) and I had chosen to surprise him at the local driving range. We had never been before and I know he was interested in trying it. I had booked it for 10am but with the crazy morning with kids and school, we were running late. Old anxious me would have been so anxious about being late and pushing myself to get there at 10am, sharp! But the new me knew to just take my time and get there safely and as best as I could. We arrived about 25 minutes late and thankfully we did because all the earlier morning guests were leaving. We had the whole place to ourselves!! It was amazing! We had so much fun just goofing around and enjoying the experience. Had we come on time we would have been with many others and it would have been crowded! How's that for letting it just flow and letting go of control!

Let's put this into another perspective. Some time ago I was at work and had been asked to organise catering for an event that was happening in the next week. I had been so busy that day (a Friday), that I forgot to do it! I woke up in the middle of the night stressing about all the worst-case scenarios and letting everyone down. The next day I tried to call around all the catering venues but being a Saturday they were all closed! I was so anxious all weekend that when Monday rolled around I called the venue up in a stress panic, only to find out that one of my team members had already alerted them about it a few weeks ago and they were only just waiting on some final information from us! They were all across it, and were going to contact my work that day anyway! So here I was anxious all weekend about something that had been ok. I just didn't have all the information yet. When I hit the roadblock on Saturday with all the venues being closed, I just needed to have faith that it would work out and put it to the side until Monday.

Now the above situations may not seem like big deals to most people. I can give you examples of when I have leaned into faith big time! Like quitting full-time steady jobs without having an income stream to fall back on, plenty of debt and no new job to go to, and then like magic, as soon as I make the big leap of faith and quit, something pops up not long after. I have had many of these big leap of faith moments in the past but at this part of the anxiety journey, I was not ready to start doing those yet! I needed something I could work with for now. I had to practice faith in small doses before jumping without knowing that no matter what this part of the journey looked like, I would be ok!

I had to learn it was ok to let go of the need to control and it was safe to lean into faith. Over time I learned that by stepping back for a few moments we leave ourselves open to explore new ideas, explore new solutions, and we have time for new information to drop in.

I often affirm to myself, "I will do the best I can with what I have right now, and I have faith that it will turn out ok soon."

Worrying and stressing with anxiety burns up so much energy and time. I read somewhere once that went something a little like this: *"There is no point worrying about something twice!"* E.g. before it happens and then again if it even happens. This always rang true to me and I remind myself of this when I come to these blocks.

TRY THIS:
Well by now you have probably worked out that I love games right? These obstacles, stop signs, or 'dirty laundry' moments are great opportunities for mind-flip games and practising faith! Whilst this is a good time to revisit the '*What Can Go Right game*', I do have another game in the arcade.

This one I refer to as the **'Road Less Travelled' game.** Often when we want to take leaps of faith down a new path at a fork in the road, we can get anxious or scared and want to run back to our usual comfort zones. This new game starts to implant the idea that it's safe to take new paths. It's simple. Next time you go for a drive, a walk, or any other way of travel to a destination, even if it's one you do all the time, take a new path to get there. Take a little extra time to discover a new route no matter if it takes longer than usual, even if you get lost. Take a new street. Go to a new playground with the kids. Go to a different beach, lake, or walking trail. On the way to work explore the back roads to get to the same destination. Explore! Get used to doing things differently in your usual day. If you can't do it with travel do it in the way you go about your usual routines. Do them differently. Eat dessert before dinner or cook a meal you have never attempted before. The point is to get your mind on board with doing things different to the way you have done them previously and to start thinking about your steps in a new way, not the autopilot way!

I told a friend once I bet I could come up with 10 different ways to hand wash the dirty dishes, and yes I did! I would do them while dancing, I would change the side of the sink I used, I would wear my bikini and splash water everywhere, I would change the order in which I did them e.g. plates then cups then utensils or the other way round. I could even do it blindfolded, on one leg, talking in different voices or doing 3 squats between each dish! So, do you get my point? There are unlimited amounts of ways you can do anything! Have faith that you can solve any situation different to the way you have done before!

Dare to be different! Have faith in yourself!!

13

Responsibility

RESPONSIBILITY FOR ME, MYSELF, I, AND OF COURSE, MY ANXIETY OVER THERE

" I had lost so much trust in myself and let my anxiety rule my life." - Amy J Young

Oh responsibility! It's like discipline's older sibling. Another word that anxiety and I did not like. The last thing I wanted was more responsibility that I had to worry about. That was until I understood what responsibility really meant to me personally, and not just what I was taught in school.

Here I will be touching on only one layer of how deep responsibility can go. You would have noticed that in this book so far I haven't spoken about other people and their roles in my anxiety journey. I understand and I know first-hand that there are often people in our lives who are not supportive or kind to what you may be going through. We are not responsible or in control of others' actions, thoughts or feelings. Only our own. However, the thing about responsibility and any inner work is always starting, and ending, with you. The most important person in your life. Like with forgiveness, I start with the self before moving on to look at others. Responsibility is no different.

There are two parts to responsibility as I see it.

One:
You have control over every thought, feeling and action you make, whether consciously or unconsciously. Period. You hold the responsibility, and the power to do this.

What has happened in the past is not always a direct fault of your own. I know that we don't always put ourselves into specific situations purposely and can be caught up in an experience we never wanted or intended. What you choose to do going forward in relation to your thoughts, feelings and actions, however, is your responsibility. Blaming others for your anxiety is only going to keep you holding on to the anxiety. For the anxiety to become less, take full responsibility for your anxiety going forward. This is YOUR anxiety and this is YOUR life. You get to choose how this will play out from this moment on.

Two:
It is your responsibility and yours alone to work with your anxiety. Others can help, can guide, support and encourage you but at the end of the day it's up to you to keep yourself accountable for your actions and your journey.

Taking ownership of your anxiety is giving you back your power. Holding on to the past is giving that power away. I never dismiss that other people or situations could be part of why someone experiences anxiety, it most definitely can, but what I do know is that taking back the power by owning MY anxiety now helps me realise that the power over this from now on is mine. My feelings! My thoughts! My anxiety! In the last chapter, we discussed faith and how we are not in control of everything in life, but we are the masters of our own feelings, thoughts, and actions.

This is what we do get to choose in life. This is power. We no longer need to let anxiety run the show and take over. But how you may ask? Anxiety always takes over my whole being and when it has a hold of me I can no longer function until it has passed! Well, we remember that anxiety is our responsibility, and just as any parent would do with their child, we gently guide it back to safety. Remember the Triangle Trigger back in part one? I tune in and ask my anxiety about what is going on. What triggered me? What is out of balance right now? Anxiety is showing me that something is not quite right and it is my responsibility to work with my mind, body, and soul so that I am back in balance. By doing this I am taking back my power from my anxiety and remembering that it is not the boss.

I am the one who decides how I feel, act, and think. I am my own responsibility and my anxiety is just one part of me - this incredible yet beautifully complex human being. I call the shots for me!

Rise up, Anxiety Warrior! Take back your power! I see you and I most definitely believe in you!

TRY THIS:
The only exercise I can give you here is to practice talking to your anxiety and reminding it who holds the responsibility. Practice gently guiding it back to balance. Check-in with what is triggering you right now. What is out of balance and how can you lovingly guide yourself

back? It may be as simple as just breathing, or doing something that brings you joy, removing yourself from a certain situation for the time being. Be patient like a parent to their little one while you practice this part. It's not always simple to just switch from highly anxious to the boss. Be gentle through the process of change.

Before moving on I want to share something that I wrote several years ago, about my son Zephyr, when he was 4 years old. It helps me understand balance, responsibility and meeting our needs.

Dear Anxiety,
Zephyr's mission every day is to have fun. It is the first thing he thinks about when he gets up and it is the thing he fights for until he falls asleep. He told me that his favourite thing to do is play. It's all he ever wants to do and asks me over and over to play together.

I don't mind as we play very imaginative games out of anything we can find. We play very silly, over the top and make up our own rules to the game as we go along.

When he is upset or if I ask him why he did something, it usually comes down to seeking play and joy. He may not understand the concept of responsibility the way I might perceive it as an adult but for him, he believes it is his only responsibility in life to seek and have fun.

I know I can learn from this! As an adult, I often forget that play, fun and joy can be the reason why we do many things in life. Yes, responsibility actually can be fun! As long as our play, fun and joy is with heart and not at the expense of another. Why shouldn't we continue the mission of seeking play in our day as an adult? Would this help with so many of the feelings we have bottled up? Wouldn't this help take off so much pressure in our day?

Children can be our biggest teachers!

14

Love

LOVE ANXIETY? IS THAT EVEN POSSIBLE?

The thing about my anxiety was that it was unpredictable. I never knew how far it was going to go. Was I going to black out, find myself in the arms of some stranger on the doctor's surgery floor feeling completely embarrassed, or was I going to lose complete control? And yes, I did faint in a doctor's surgery waiting room once!

I lost the ability to trust myself. I lost the ability to be able to control myself. I lost the ability to feel ok being me. These three things were a recipe for dark thoughts and the loss of motivation for pretty much life in general. I had some very dark times which I would hide from family and friends as I didn't want anyone to worry about me. I didn't think anyone would even understand, so I just coasted through what I could. I put on a brave face and pushed myself harder in my work so I didn't have to deal with myself, or worse, my feelings! I would shield away from certain situations that I knew would set me off and replace them with a busy lifestyle. This would work for a little while. It would keep me occupied from having to address my own needs. I stopped thinking or caring about myself and I often forgot even how to! I only ate when

I remembered or was in front of people, and it wasn't always the best choice of food. I lived on caffeine and sugar to keep me going. I was an insomniac through most of the night. I lost a lot of weight and struggled to put any on.

A week before my wedding my dressmaker told me I needed to put weight on so that I could fit my dress in a week! She had already downsized it as much as possible and there was no way it could get smaller! That week I ate a lot of unhealthy foods, thinking this would work, and I ended up feeling sick, rundown and with cold sores on my lips on my wedding day. I was devastated and so down on myself, on what was meant to be one of the happiest days of my life! Thank goodness for make-up! I felt so unhealthy. Even though the day was perfect in every other way and I had an incredibly supportive husband who loved me no matter what I looked like, it took me a while to forgive myself for treating myself the way I had.

As I started to work with love I knew the time had come to finally address how I was treating myself. Both physically and mentally. Physically, I didn't care for my body much, and mentally, I didn't prioritise care for myself and my needs. At this stage, I was starting to write articles about anxiety and I was asked by a friend to write about self-love. Self-love was the new buzzword at this time and everyone was talking about it. (Rightfully so I might add!)

I realised then, that I had no idea what self-love for myself even was! I was dumbfounded that I had never actually even contemplated what it was like to ask myself what I needed or what love was. Did I even love myself? It felt so foreign. It still amazes me that I managed in all my years to not think about myself like this. It took me a while to complete my self-love piece and I would often sit at an empty screen just staring at it and feeling perplexed. That was until one day my true thoughts finally streamed through.

I want to share it with you in this book and I have included it below. This piece of writing changed the way I thought about myself and set into motion asking myself deeper questions. I immediately felt I needed to love myself more, and that included every part of me including my anxiety. Particularly even more so when I was anxious! I needed my love more than anything!

Dear Anxiety,

I love how there is a self-love topic at the forefront of many magazines, social media posts and online articles. I love that it is finally becoming the topic of a number of conversations between so many. However I have to be honest, I have never quite understood what self-love means.

Sure I have had thoughts about what it is and can only assume what I think it is but as I sit down to write this I find myself scratching my head as to what it really means to love myself.

So I will start here. There are days when I look in the mirror and I think, hmmm, ok, I look nice today and there are days when I cannot stand to even look at myself. So is this self-love? Being ok with what is reflected in the mirror? Maybe but surely it's more than that.

What if we go deeper? What is behind the clothes, the hair, the make-up? A human body. Do I love this body? Hmm, it's ok? If I loved it more would this be self-love? Maybe.

What is behind the body? Organs, muscles, tissues, blood. Do I love this part of my body? Sure. I'm thankful, it works in a way I don't quite understand and the design of how it all works together is nothing short of mindblowing. If I love this more is it self-love? It could be.

And behind this? Emotions, feelings, senses, thoughts. An incredible vast network of these unseen "things" that run deeply through my body. Carrying every single thought, action and memory and delivering it with lightning speed along carefully grown networks of energy within my body. Can I love this? Would this be self-love?

Can I go even deeper? Whatever could be beyond this beautiful design? Atoms, neutrons and vibrating energy may not be seen by the naked eye or even a microscope. I can't see it but I know they exist. Yes. If I love all of this would this be self-love?

Could I possibly try to go even deeper than this? What is it? I can feel it, it's like an infinite open expansiveness that feels a bit like space. But it's peaceful and it feels like, well it feels like peace. I think it feels like love. Like an unconditional type of love. I don't know how to explain it as I cannot see it with my eyes but I can feel it if I try to. I can feel it with everything that I am. It feels like love.

Can all this expansiveness be within the person that I am? All of this? If I can love all of this, every particle, every network, every blood cell, every organ, every skin cell and every single part of my connected energy. Is this self-love? Loving every single part of myself? From every thought to every action to every moment, movement and sense. If I can truly understand that myself as a whole is made of love. I truly can love and be loved! When I drop back to *the surface, my body, my clothes my hair, how can I not be in awe and in love with all of this? A whole universe inside of myself that I never knew existed but shows up as this being reflected to me in the mirror. Wow. Why wouldn't I want to take care of this amazing temple that houses this incredible expansiveness of love? This amazing well of infinite energy that feels incredible. How can I not stand here and be moved by this?*

So I want to leave you dear reader with this. It has been famously said.....'And in the end, the love you get is equal to the love you give,'...think about that for a moment. Not my quote but a famous one from a very well-known song. I may not have understood it until now.

I now understand self-love and what it means to me.

So from my heart space to yours...you will be loved.

- Amy J Young

Not too long after writing this piece, I started a small routine each day, after accidentally finding that it helped enormously!

I would have a shower at night - in candlelight!

My husband had suggested it and lit the candles for me. I don't know what it was about showering in the candlelight but I immediately felt more calm and relaxed. The warm water on my face in the almost darkness just overrode the big bold bright lights and my mind spirals. Every night I would use this time to myself to just breathe and think about this expansiveness within while I was held in this safe place in the water. I would think about what was underneath all of my top layers and imagine myself as more than just a body. I would then mentally wash all my worries away and imagine them leaving me down the shower drain. Sometimes I would cry and just let the tears also wash any heaviness away. It was a great reset before bed. It was a chance to just be me, all of me, in a safe surrounding, even if for only a few minutes. This was just a simple act of self-love that I could give to myself each day in a busy lifestyle.

Never underestimate the small things!

TRY THIS:
What act of self-love and/or care can you do for yourself each day? Even if it's only a small amount of time or effort? How can you begin to show love and care for you? Just for a few minutes each day, prioritise you! You need it more now than ever! If someone you loved was anxious, would you treat them with love and care? Absolutely! So why not you?

If you are ready, take some time to think about yourself and what lies under the surface, and have the courage to truly explore that you are so much more than what shows up in the mirror.

15

Wholeness

WE ARE ONE, BOTH MY ANXIETY AND I.

When we start to accept and understand that we are made up of so many different aspects we become whole again. We learn that anxiety is just one part of the incredible vastness that is ourselves. And like all of these amazing multi-faceted parts of our amazing selves, anxiety deserves attention and to be brought back into your whole being where it belongs.

Seeing anxiety as just one part of ourselves, we realise like all parts, it can become out of balance, exerted or has lost its way. Most times it's not always just anxiety that has walked away from being whole but sadness, anger, depression and even grief can also be working with it. You can probably even think of a whole list of other feelings that may have started siding with your anxiety. Seeing these parts of me as that, beautiful individuals unique parts, I realise they all need to be acknowledged and integrated to make me feel whole again. I could accept them as individual parts of me that need attention rather than avoiding them.

They are all just as important as the others and they all make up aspects of me that without them, I could not function optimally.

I would picture all these unique parts of me and gently bring them back into what felt like alignment. I would start with all the things I could name like anxiety, sadness, anger, fear, guilt and shame. I wasn't quite ready to deal with these heavier feelings yet but at this stage, I just wanted to acknowledge that these feelings were important and valid. I would move up the scale to more positive feelings like joy, contentedness, calmness, kindness, and happiness. This process was about accepting that I am made up of so many facets of all kinds. Some feel great and some not so great but they are all me.

TRY THIS:

Yes another game! This is a mind game I play by myself and even sometimes with my kids. The "Shiny Things" Game! I absolutely love bubbles and I also love fireworks, so I would either imagine them or draw them on a piece of paper. I would name each feeling I could and I would place a bubble or firework around it and imagine it coming back to me so it could feel whole again.

You are probably thinking that bubbles and fireworks usually go away from the person. So like all great stretching and strengthening mind games, I had to try a little harder to imagine them coming back to me. No autopiloting here! I would call back all my anxiety, and imagine them coming to be loved and held back in my heart where it was safe. This does not just have to be feelings, it could be any part of you that you feel just needs to be acknowledged or accepted and stored lovingly in your being safe again. It could be your inner child or a situation you are going through that just needs to be held. This one is a safe and not too overwhelming exercise. (I start to deal with the heavier feelings in both the Body and Soul books).

This game sets up the understanding that we are made up of so many diverse and unique parts that all deserve to be loved and feel safe.

Anxiety is just one part of you and that's ok. It is not the whole of you. You are so perfectly made up of so much more than that. Self-acceptance for who you were, who you are and who you will be is a powerful act of returning to wholeness.

16

Joy

FEELING JOY WHEN ANXIOUS

Would you ever think that joy and anxiety could work together? I remember in the days when I suffered from severe anxiety, being too joyous made me feel even more anxious. If I laughed too much or my heart rate got a little higher I would start to panic. The things I used to love doing became the things I would avoid. Like going to the movies, playing sports, riding on roller coasters or travelling on an aeroplane. There was even a time when I stopped simple things like jogging, dancing and drinking wine to going out socially. I avoided these situations because I believed I would suffer a panic attack. I thought it meant I could never be happy again. I would always have to be cautious and try to stay in control at all times.

As you can imagine life got frustrating and sad as I told myself each day that I could no longer do the things I loved. What was the point? Why bother looking forward to anything exciting anymore?

However, at the back of my mind, I always knew, and hoped, that this would pass. But the question was of time. When? When would I be cured? When could I enjoy my life again?

Over time when I learned that I was experiencing anxiety and started to implement the exercises and games in this book, I slowly realised that I was right! I can overcome this! I will be able to do the things I love again!

I decided to start small. Each day I would make a goal to incorporate something fun. I was working in a full-time job so the only time I had to myself was early in the morning. I was very fortunate to live near the ocean at the time, and I always enjoyed taking photos, so each day I planned to wake early, walk to the beach and capture my progress with my camera.

Wow! Was I surprised!

I realised that waking early meant witnessing the beauty of sunrises over the ocean. I was so proud of my photos that I began to share them with others, and every day I became so excited to wake up early and go for my walk. I realised that during these times of beauty, I was so focused on getting to the beach and capturing an image that I had very little time to think about anxiety. I started to feel safe and that it was a rewarding routine. I would also use the walk as my mindfulness meditation. I would feel each step with my feet, repeat affirmations as I moved, and take notice of as much of the beauty around me as I could. The trees, flowers, animals, ocean and more. It had always been there but now I could see it and appreciate it. It's like a whole new world had opened up to me. I felt awakened. I was full of gratitude and once again, joy!

TRY THIS:

I challenge you to schedule some time to start something small each day, a hobby you once had or always wanted to explore, e.g. reading, painting, writing, drawing, gardening, creating videos, or exploring. Make it small so it's not too overwhelming, like drawing a tree each day or taking a different kind of photo each day. It can be anything! Anything that makes you even just a little bit happy, that you can do regularly, and that does not need an outcome of any type. Just simply doing. Remember to permit yourself to be present when you do it.

17

Peace

FINDING PEACE WITH ANXIETY

When I think about Peace I originally thought that it meant to just be relaxed. A quiet mind. Feeling like I am in a peaceful place and contemptuous of life at that moment. The complete opposite of having anxiety! The complete opposite of an overstimulated mind going a million miles an hour with every worst-case scenario possible.

When I was learning about the Everyday Lightworker Principle of Peace, it opened up a whole new way of self-acceptance and enlightenment for me. To me, it finally means coming to an agreement with the anxious part of myself. It is accepting my anxiety as part of me and working with it when it pops up in my life.

As you know from reading these chapters, anxiety comes into my life when I am not meeting the needs of my mind, body and/or soul. I find when I am tired, burnt out, or overwhelmed my anxiety holds up the little red flag to make me notice that I need to stop, breathe, tune in, and listen. I sometimes picture my anxious self as a 'little peacemaker' who jumps in when my head and heart are in disagreement. There is anxiety, in the middle of my fighting head and heart, trying to bring all parties to a stop. Seeing anxiety this way, as a peacemaker, is not the way others may describe it but I do believe that my anxiety is looking out for me.

Accepting anxiety as a blessing in my life and learning to love this part of me has been life-changing. Working with each of these chapters from Honesty, where I was at my absolute lowest point, all the way to Peace, has changed my outlook on anxiety. From the beginning, I thought I had to cure it completely, but after the journey through the Everyday Lightworker Principles, from Honesty to Peace, I realised I only needed to embrace it!

These days I hardly experience anxiety, but occasionally it is known to sometimes tap me on the shoulder or whisper in my ear when I am in need of some self-care. It is never as scary as it used to be and I am no longer afraid of it.

A practice I once used to feel more at peace with my anxiety was to write down all the things about anxiety I was grateful for. Not your usual gratitude work as this was specifically thanks to anxiety! This process helped me to embrace anxiety and to be thankful for having been on this journey, hand in hand.

I was thankful for how it taught me self-care and self-acceptance. I learned how to open my mind, change my thought patterns and learned how to truly understand what it is like to feel still and present. It helped me to make the major changes in my life that in the past I was too afraid of.

I had a better understanding of fear and how to truly care for my mind, body, and soul. I no longer try to avoid myself or my feelings.

Anxiety helped me to discover my passions of writing and photography, two things that I wouldn't have started to work on without the beautiful help of anxiety!

But most of all, I am thankful that anxiety has taught me to be ME! I am finally at peace with being myself and for the first time in my life, I understand who I am. I had finally found peace with the most important person in my life – ME. I have anxiety to thank for that.

TRY THIS:

Write or find a quiet place to sit and list to yourself reasons you may be thankful for your anxiety. You can use some of the examples I have used above if you need help. Writing is a great way or you can just say them out loud if you prefer. It helps to be in a quiet relaxed state. Remember anxiety is a part of you and deserves to be loved just as you do. Can you find peace with anxiety? I hope you can. After all, it is in the end, you, and you are the only peacemaker in your life.

18

Outwards

If you are still with me dear reader and have made it this far through the book, thank you! Well done! Maybe you gave all the chapters a go? Maybe you tried only a few? Either way, I am thankful you have read to the end here.

This book - The Mind, is just the first part of the triangle I spoke about at the beginning and will be followed by two very different books, The Body, and The Soul. They are not written the same as The Mind as I believe each component is just as beautifully complex, and naturally, deserves its own unique approach.

Working with the Mind to support it being in a more positive state is incredibly helpful to be able to take on the deeper and inner work of The Body and The Soul. Becoming more aware of our thoughts and learning to work WITH our anxiety rather than against it, is the key to longer times without it.

At the beginning of this book, I wrote about anxiety being a Superpower. Anxiety can be described as many things like a feeling, a symptom, a condition – but most likely never a Superpower!

Of course, in the early years, I would have described it only as my archnemesis!

After much inner work and implementing many support tools like the ones in this book, I realised it was my wake-up call and the answer to everything I wanted in life. Anxiety was the catalyst that forced me to finally go within. To listen to what I really wanted, and needed, in life. To learn who I truly was and to show me how I could become the best version of myself that I truly desired. I wanted to be that incredible authentic version for so long but I constantly self-sabotaged myself with my unconscious patterns, beliefs and programming. Anxiety was that little peacekeeper, that little whisper in the ear to let me know that I was out of balance and needed attention. I needed to face myself if I wanted to change.

When I tuned in and listened to my anxiety I slowly became stronger. When I replaced my fearful thoughts with more positive ones, I became stronger. When I used the incredible energy bursts that came with the flight or fight response and channelled it into something positive, you guessed it, I became stronger. I would feel that energy within and call it that, my superpower! At first, I was afraid of it, but then I started to use it for doing something positive, like writing, photography, and visually experiencing and taking in the natural beauty that surrounded me. I found I could turn it from fear to excitement! Yes, excitement! (I will explain more in the next book)!

Both physically and mentally my anxiety brought me back to what I needed to work on within myself to build my strength. This is my superpower. Only I can wield and harness this power within. And as they say, with great power comes great responsibility. My anxiety is my responsibility. My life is my responsibility. One that I will now happily take on knowing that it is the pathway to the change I want to create for me. And when I am working on a better version of myself, the people I love and care for can be inspired too. They get the real me and I get to discover how incredible the real me is!

My whole world opens up and the possibilities become endless.

Anxiety is a superpower!

Dear Reader,

I can't wait to share with you how to support The Body through anxiety in the next Anxiety Diaries book. It is a whole other level, full of new and very creative exercises to support you on your journey!

Until then, I wish you the best through your anxiety. There is no failing with anxiety, only new layers to meeting the incredible person you are.

Thank you for sharing your time with me and reading this book.

Lots of love,

Amy

Resources

THE 12 EVERYDAY LIGHTWORKER PRINCIPLES

For more information about these incredible Everyday Lightworker Principles please check out the following resources. They have helped me enormously and I am very thankful to Michelle Lightworker and the Lightworker Practitioner family.

Podcast
Everyday Lightworker 101 by Michelle Lightworker

Online Magazine - available on Issu
Lightworker Advocate

www.ingramcontent.com/pod-product-compliance
Lightning Source LLC
Chambersburg PA
CBHW062112290426
44110CB00023B/2790